My
Heart's
Delight

Love Within

Annika Jones-Gonzales

Order this book online at www.trafford.com
or email orders@trafford.com

Most Trafford titles are also available at major online book retailers.

Printed in the United States of America.

ISBN: 978-1-4669-0752-2 (sc)
ISBN: 978-1-4669-0754-6 (hc)
ISBN: 978-1-4669-0753-9 (e)

Library of Congress Control Number: 2011962297

Trafford rev. 01/19/2012

 www.trafford.com

North America & international
toll-free: 1 888 232 4444 (USA & Canada)
phone: 250 383 6864 ✦ fax: 812 355 4082

This book is dedicated to three very important women in my life; Mama Flo, Patricia and Tina Gonzales. You all touched my life in a beautiful way.
You were Angels here on earth, though you were called home you will never be forgotten. I cherish the moments we've shared and forever hold on to our memories. Until we see each other again,
I Love You.

First and foremost, I would like to thank God for blessing me with a gift that I didn't realize I had. It wasn't until He placed others in my path that appreciated my ability to write. He spoke to me through my sister Debbie and my dear friend Robin. I thank you both for encouraging me to utilize my gift. I'd also like to thank Charles and Laquieta Cooks for your trust and support.

My father, Lee Jones, for taking on the responsibility of being a wonderful Dad. The morals you have instilled in us and the love you've given are far more appreciated than words can say. To my three beautiful children and two grandchildren, I love you unconditionally. I am grateful for my family and friends for caring, loving and understanding. You are all greatly appreciated.

CONTENTS

A WOMAN'S WORTH

He Comforts Her With His Entirety
He Understands Her Inside and Out Completely
He Is In Touch With His Emotions
He Is Not Ashamed, Scared Of
But Goes Through The Motions
He Protects Her, He's Devoted, And Divine
The Love They Have For Each Other Is Intertwined

They Become One, Nothing Breaks Them Undone
He Is Determined Until Kingdom Comes
The Rumors, The Jealousy, The Hate, The Envy
They Are In Touch With One Another, He's Had An Epiphany
Never To Listen To Others Trying To Break Them Apart
For He Is True, They Are Complete, She Holds His Heart
But Most Importantly, The Lord Jesus Christ Is Their Rock

WHO AM I

Who am I ~As far as the human eye can see
Who am I ~As far as the human flesh wants me to be
Who am I ~What anyone wants me to be
Who am I ~No, they don't really know me
Who am I ~Some say I'm high sidity but nah that doesn't bother me
Who am I ~I am a mommy & granny
Who am I ~My family and friends accept me for me
Who am I . . . For I am me . . .

SELF WOMAN

She Stands On Top Of Her World
Looking Through The Windows Of Her Soul
And Knows She's Worthy . . .
Well Intact With Her Mind, Body and Spirit
Guarding Her Heart, Aware Not To Let The Wrong Come Near
Putting All of Her Trust In God
For He Is The Only One She Trusts
With Every Cell In Her Body
He Lifts Her Up, Loving Her Unconditionally
Whispering To Her, Guiding Her, Making
Her Aware Of Her Surroundings
She Grasps On To It All, She Stands Strong, Not To Fall
Never Losing Her Dignity, I Say It Loud, I Say It Proud
For She Is ME . . .

A GENTLE MAN

Whether he's a seven, six or five If he's willing to dive
in to get to know me without all the jive but thrive

what could be if he opens up to let me in
our love will be so very Strong & beautiful

we both will carry each other's hearts secure eventually to
marry
to label or put a number on him is unnecessary though on the
contrary

he may be an eight but if he holds the key that opens the
gate
to love me it'll never be too late

within me If he's a nine, fine & willing to dine
that truth will come out in time
the ultimate is a ten he'll communicate, understand & cherish
my whole being

BEHIND EVERY MAN STANDS A STRONG WOMAN

Dear Heavenly Father Can You Hear Me
I'm Reaching Out To You To Help Protect My Family

The Love We Have For You Is So Divine
We Stand Together Spine To Spine

Love So Great Yours, Theirs & Mine
Please Cover, Protect & Shelter Us

With Our Hearts Entirety We Trust
That This Storm & Troubled Time Too Will Bust

We Praise You, Your Mercy and Your Grace
That We Will Get Through This Troubled Place

When You Arrive At Your Time To Come
We Will Be Let Into Heaven To Honor You
Face to Face

GEM

~I am a Woman, I am a Gem, I LOVE ALL OF ME WITHIN, I am to be RESPECTED, I am not to be USED, So PLEASE don't get the two CONFUSED, Don't play with my HEART, Don't toy with my Mind, I am surely one of a Kind...I am a Woman, I am a Gem, I LOVE ALL OF ME & THE SKIN I'M IN~

SISTER LOVE

I miss you already I missed you before we left the drive way
I often call you my twin because we are so much alike, outside
and in

You are my shine to my light my sweet to my nectar
our relationship couldn't get any better

You understand me whole I think God made me out of your
mold
I love you so much when I hear your voice I can also feel your
touch

When I'm feeling down and blue you say just the right thing
to make me feel brand new we are sisters forever I will leave
you never

 ♥ ♥ ♥ I LOVE YOU ♥ ♥ ♥

FOREVER MY FRIEND

Friends may come and friends may go
You'll be in my heart always this you should know

Friends are different like flakes of snow
You know every inch of me from head to toe

You never try to put on a show just being you surrounded by
your glow
From the moment I met you to eternity I'll never let you go

I LOVE YOU

I love you like honey loves bees
I love you like pollen loves the trees
I love you like sweet loves the spoon
I love you like night loves the moon
I love you like bright loves the sun
I love the thoughts of you that flow through
My mind on my daily run
I love you like wet loves the rain
I love you like blood loves the vein
I love you like colors love the rainbow
I love every inch of you from temple to toe
I love you

WHISPER

Whisper in my sleep, Whisper when I'm awake
Whisper for Peace, Whisper for Goodness sake
Whisper when I'm down and Out, Whisper when I want to shout
Whisper to gain peace of mind, Whisper your one of a kind
Whisper when I'm lost and scared, Whisper thanks for being there
Whisper what you want me too, Whisper I Love you too

VALENTINE SWEET VALENTINE

Valentine Sweet Valentine
So We Meet Again

You Staying Around This Time
Or You Here To Befriend, HA HA!

Your Smooth Operations, Thinking Your So Fine
How You Combine Your Slickness, The Way You

Wine And Dine, Filling Me Up With That Brandywine
Whispering In My Ear, Fingers Lightly Caressing

Mine, Making Sure Our Bodies Become Intertwined
Your Masculinity, Rubbing All Over Me, Telling Me

There's No Other Place You'd Rather Be, But Naw
That Won't Work This Time, For Now I See

So Take Your Dreadful Games, I'm Tired Of The Lame
Everything Always The Same Ole Same
Don't Look My Way, Keep Swaying On By
You Can Keep All Your Lullabies

No, You Can't get Over, I'm Much Wiser And Older
I'm Gonna Wait, On My Strong True Soldier

I BELIEVE

I believe that your smile is like the rays from the sunshine
I believe that your eyes sparkle like the bubbly in
my cherry wine
I believe that your kiss reminds me of sweet caramel
mocha that blows my mind
I believe that your love exceeds the hurtful kind
I believe that true love is surely hard to find

HONEY DEW

Sweet as honey dew, your intellect, calmness and smile
Draws me closer to you all the pleasures of your glow
Rolled up locked tight like a tootsie roll
An inhale of your essence the thought of your presence
As the room lights up at the sight of your entrance
Cherry Blossom letters leave your lips as you
Complete your sentence when you whisper to me
"I LOVE YOU"

PROTECT US FROM EVIL

Yes, We Are A Close-Knit Family
We Stand Strong Keeping Out The Enemy
The Foundation Was Set Way Back In Century
It Was Instilled In Us That's The Way It's Supposed To Be
It's True We May Fuss And Fight
The Bond We Share It Holds Steady
True With All It's Might
The Saying Is Water Isn't As Thick As Blood
When The Storms Come In We Block The Flood
The Evil, The Hate, The Envy, Tries To Bust Through Our
Gate
Though We Won't Let Them Use Us As Bait
Our Faith, Love & Belief Will Set Them Straight
That Surely As Our Love Is Pure For Jesus
The Enemy Will Surely Deflate

MY MAHOGANY SOLDIER

Beautiful was your skin at first sight
Body so perfect just right
Your intellect philosophy heart so pure
Was more than I could endure
You swept me off my feet
My heart never skipped a beat
Our brief sweet love affair
No other man could ever compare
Your chiseled arms your chest and muscles
Woven around the rest of you
Now what am I supposed to do
You're just a memory
My Mahogany Soldier

MY IMAGINATION

I close my eyes, my imagination takes me there,
To a place so gentle, so free, no pain, no worries,
Children jumping on the clouds, sliding down the rainbows,
all smiles and laughter
No fear, just peace
It's up above, above and beyond
Let your mind go with me

I use my imagination to take me there, to a place so free, at
peace,
I walk around jumping from cloud to cloud
I dive into the deep blue ocean body moving freely with every
motion
I run to the rainbow, glaring at the sun glow, down on me, my
mind at peace, so free

ME, MY OWN QUEEN

Don't worry about the way I dress, for,
I'm not here to impress, you,
Though I must confess, that I rock the best,

From my hair to my shoes, getting dressed singing the blues,
High notes, in notes, and in between,
I am a Queen
None like me foreseen around me, I be who I be
My Own Queen

CONCENTRATE

You say "AROUND THE WAY," I say: MOTIVATE, DEDICATE, CONCENTRATE & NEVER HUMILIATE, IMPERSONATE, JUST BE A BEDMATE-IT COMPLICATES! MANIPULATE, DICTATE OR INTERROGATE, AFFILIATE with NEGATIVITY but ELIMINATE IT, LET THAT EVAPORATE! CAN'T ABBREVIATE OR DUPLICATE ME BUT NAVIGATE TO POSITIVITY TO APPRECIATE, CALCULATE, CELEBRATE, HYDRATE, EXHILARATE! ELATE EACH OTHER WITH LOVE..MUST BE FATE

MOTHERSHIP

Embedded Is The Seed That Lays There To Manifest
Worry, Wonder & Fear Standfast As She Lays In The Nest
Groped Is The Shell That Surrounds And Protects
Though It's The Mothership That Holds The Rest
She Must Hold On To Faith To Keep Out All Evil & Harm That
Awaits
The Darkness Will Be Dwindled by God's Grace

ME FOR ME

I'm sitting here marinating in my worst fear
to open again hoping you'd remain my friend

Though I wish I could feel your touch I want to so much
I know you feel differently & I want you to remain friendly

I see your face it reminds me I need to give you your space
for we will never be I'd hoped you could see me for me

If that's not the case as long as I'll be able to see your face
friends we will be just accept me for me

BUTTERFLY KISSES

Butterfly Kisses I Miss As I Sit And Reminisce
The Times We Shared Were Oh So Bliss
The Only Thing Left Is Behind My Closed Eyes
Though When I Open Them
The Only Reflection I See
Is Mine Staring Back At Me
You Will Forever Be
My Memory
I Will Hold On To Those Butterfly Kisses
Every Night As I Lay To Sleep

DREAMER

For I am dreamer,
I walk through the trees, leaves roughing in the wind
I float from cloud to cloud, sliding down the rainbows,
I dance to the beat of the rain hitting the street,
I dive into the big blue sea, just to be free—For I'm a
dreamer

ANNIKA'S LULLABY

I Watch As It's Fading Away
Never Ever Will I Beg You To Stay
You Proclaim We'll Find A Way
It's Not The First Time Nor Second I've Heard You Say
But The Fifth No Sixth I'll Add If I May I Free My Mind
My Head I Lay Blessed If I Wake Tomorrow
Will Be A Brighter Day

A FATHER'S LOVE

Cheyanne, you choose your father, Steve the moment you were conceived
You choose your mother Desirae to birth you, into Earth

You are almost identical made in your father's image, not a flaw nor a blemish
He cherished you, played with you, kept you from harms way

He did this every second of your life each and everyday
He came to earth and completed what he was sent to do

Though he's home now, his love lives on through you, doing so all the while He kept everyone around him laughing, Impacting a smile

Through the clouds and rainbows, somewhere far above the mountain top,
His love will come shower you with every rain drop

FIRST

A Woman Must Put Her Self-Worth First
He Should Want Her Love & Crave His Thirst For Her
Her Love From Within To Shine Loud & Bright
She Should Hold The Glow To His Light Never To Let Anyone
Get The Best
She Should Come Before The Rest
She Should Be Cherished & Loved Back Equally Not Underneath
Or In Between
So Clear It Is Seen That Her Wants & Needs Matter As Does His
Together Their Love Will Be Bliss
(Never be held on by a string shoved in the back pocket or front
for that matter
to be a "if all else fails" or "I know she'll pickup"
BUT FIRST)

HE HOLDS HER

HE HOLDS HER UP ON TOP OF HIS WORLD
SHE IS HIS PERFECT ANGEL A BEAUTIFUL WOMAN
THEY INTERTWINE AS ONE THE WAY IT SHOULD BE DONE
MEN TREAT WOMEN WELL LOVE HER RESPECT HER FOR
SHE IS FRAGILE
WOMEN STAND BY HIS SIDE SHOW HIM RESPECT LOVE HIM
WHOLEHEARTEDLY TOGETHER THEY REPRESENT THE
TOTALITY OF GOD

LOST

How can I fall in love with someone I don't even know
Aren't I supposed to know him first so our love can grow
If he has love for me, it will also show
But still I love him whole from head to toe
The way he makes me feel, oh and his touch
When I'm not with him I long for him so much
His kiss, his smell, the way he looks
The daggers in me, deep down tightened like hooks
He sits me on top of him, deeply I take his love in
We stare into each others eyes the true love I feel within
His lips so soft as he kisses me passionately
My mind, my soul is willingly, happily
For our bodies to become as one
At that moment we will let nothing break us undone
I'm willing to accept him, his flaws & all
Because I'm wise enough to know at some point we all fall
My mind so confused I don't know what to do
Don't know if it's a dream or can it all be true
I ask myself do I let go or see it through
Can this be the beginning of something new

WISE

My Daddy Taught Us to Love No Matter the Skin They're In
To Remember Our Morales & Accept the Person and Love for
What Lies Within
My Mother Taught Us Girls that a Man Will Tell You Anything
to Get In
But to remember the fact that he will only Love you if he's a
Gentleman
And to Be Wise to an Associate and Who is Really a Friend
Nonetheless I have Captured Both Their Words &
Live Them as We Speak from Beginning to End
THANK YOU DAD & MOM

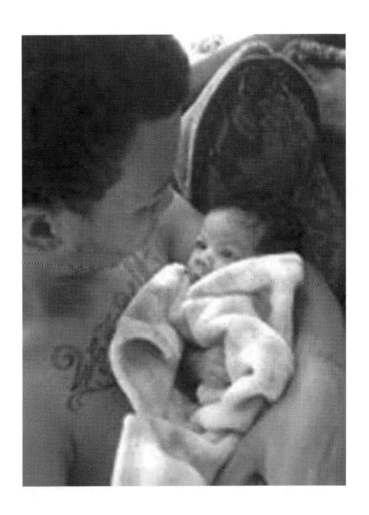

TRUE TO YOU

It's the Ones that Understand You, Accept You,
Never Hold a Grudge or Pass Judgment that Really Matter
You can still be Cordial, Keep the Peace & be Kind,
As long as you're Aware & Know Where to Place Them in Your Mind
Where They Stand, Never to Give Them the Upper Hand BUT it's a Must to Acknowledge the REAL because Truly Behind you They Stand

WE STRUGGLE TO BE WE

We Struggled For Centuries Being Declared Independence
They Freed Our Wrist From Chains
And Wrapped Them Around The Perimeter Of Our Brains
Illusioned By Fast Money And Drugs We Forgot Who We Was
More Than Athletes And Entertainers (The Original Kings Of The World)
I Tell All My Sisters They Are Queens But They Take The Position
OF Young Teenage Girls
I've Seen My Father Lose Patience With My Mother
I've Seen My Mother Help Poison Her Brother
I Learned From My Father How Not To Stick Around
I Learned From My Mother How To Hold Her Brother Down
And I'm Disappointed At My Mother's Brother
For Not Leaving A Role Model Around
I'm Exhausted From What I've Seen Consistently I've Become
All Three
Until I Fix ME
WE WILL ALWAYS STRUGGLE TO BE WE
Used by permission from: Rogelio Sealey
MY BEAUTIFUL NEPHEW

PROTOTYPE

I am the prototype of what it is to be
A strong single mother, oh I know there are plenty others
But the Lord blessed me with my three,
Jake, Aja and Boogie, I gave birth to them you see
The coughs, bumps, cuts and bruises that made them cry
The first day of school for each, the kisses and goodbyes
Getting up at midnight, breaking up the fights
Always protecting them, not letting them out of sight
One handsome boy and two beautiful girls
They make me the happiest woman in the world
I am a prototype of what is to be, a strong single mother
Holding it down, yea that's me

POSITIVELY

I do all that I must to the best of my ability..I cannot foresee
the unseen nor
unknown therefore I can only remain Positive in Everything
I do to receive a
Great Outcome positively

CLOUDS I SEE

Some people don't understand what I see or feel when I look
into the sky,
It's my outlet per say my Peace of Mind
You see, I owe Our Heavenly Father EVERYTHING
Despite all the mistakes I've made and all that I've done
I long to be there when Kingdom comes
As far as Heaven is away from the earth . . . Jesus has
protected me ever since before birth . . . This I know ♥

ASK

~Don't assume who I be, just ask ME..I'm the one who holds
the key to the best answer about Me..I Be Who I Be~

FOCUSED

~Beautiful, sexy, sweet was the taste of the morning dew..as
it kissed my lips..My mind replaying the shadowing figures
that invaded my brain the night prior to..But I won't let that
stop me in doing what I have to do~♥ FOCUSED ♥

FEELING BLUE

~YOU THOUGHT THE LOVE BETWEEN THE TWO OF YOU
WAS TRUE, THOUGH OVER AND OVER AGAIN HE KEPT YOU
FEELING BLUE
WHY PUT YOURSELF THROUGH THE MISERY
OH BEAUTIFUL ONE, FOR YOU MUST SEE
THAT YOU ARE FAR MORE WORTHY THAN HE~

DWELL NOT

What Should've been, Could've been —> Would've been
BUT Is Not..Everything you promised me I haven't forgot..
now that I look back on it ..you played me a lot..I continually
denied it to give you a shot..all along knowing what had
been on the spot ..What Would've been, Could've been, and
Should've been is Not

MY LIFE

As I sit back and study my Life
I wouldn't have had it any other way
My children keep me Striving, Motivated, Happy
Furthermore thriving everyday
I'm very thankful to God for the strength He has laid upon me
If it weren't for He who knows where we would be

AT PEACE

For She Is At Peace Within Herself
She Stares Underneath Her Eyes Music Whistling In Her
Ears By Butterflies

Her Mind, Body & Soul She Meditates
Trying Not To Think About The Hate And What They Stole
From Her

With That They Can't Get Though She Craves Her Own Self
Righteousness
This One She'll Surely Take To The Grave She Knows One
Day What Will Come

Now It's Impossible To Become Undone
Waiting Patiently Wanting To Be The Voice For Many

She Remains Silent Lying There Gently
It's Written All Over Her Face For The Whole Wide World To
See
And Still She Holds Down Her Self Dignity

BEAUTY FROM WITHIN

Beauty comes in different shapes
Beauty is different sizes, Beauty is mesmerizing
Beauty is fantasizing, Beauty is right in front of you
Beauty is right behind you, Beauty is at your side
Beauty cannot hide, Beauty starts from the inside

Beauty is not jealously, Beauty is not envy
Beauty is not conniving, Beauty is not despising
Beauty never dies, Beauty comes from Within
Beauty doesn't lie

BLIND

I WAS BLIND, GREW WISE, NOW I SEE . . . THIS IS THE WAY IT'S SUPPOSED TO BE . . . TO UNDERSTAND, HOLD & LOVE ME . . . I WILL DO THE SAME, DEFINITELY . . . STAND BY MY SIDE THROUGH THICK AND THIN, O.N.E H.U.N.D.R.E.D % TO THE END . . . PATIENCE IS VIRTUE, TRUE INDEED, FOR IF IT'S GOING TO HAPPEN . . . IT WAS MEANT TO BE

ENTICE

You entice, and nibble and bite me but still I can't lose my
dignity

But it feels so dang good just like you knew it would
I say to you I should if I could and I could if I would, but I
won't

I stand my ground
What you're doing is profound, you see
Why do you think you have to do this thing, you do to me

You pull up my skirt
And I tell you it hurts
That is my heart,
Cause you knew from the start

You weren't about me, so why should I lose my dignity

FANTASY MAN

I want a man who is nice & sweet a prince that
Lifts me off my feet swiftly in the air of the cool summer
breeze
Long walks hand in hand along the beach
Gazing into my eyes, he tells me he loves me
Cold salt water waves crashing on the shore
Lays rose peddles across the floor yellow, red & pink the
kind I adore
Cooks my favorite food, steak & lobster awaits as I walk
through the door
He hands me a glass, Pinot Grigio ready to pour
Every unisec, second & minute I love him more & more
I know he's out there somewhere I know this for sure

AN ANGEL
(GIFT FROM GOD)

So eloquently a design, So precise and defined
A creation that God created
A duplicate can never be duplicated

Your Spirit is so open and free
It glows so bright, hard for
The human eye to see

You truly are an Angel here on earth
A Precious Gift delivered from the moment of birth

Strong Willed, Strong Minded with Grace
All of you, we surely embrace

A Gift from God born precious and new
Who ever knew I would cross paths with a woman like you

NOW I SEE

Don't Reminisce On The Past There's a Reason Why It Didn't
Last
It All Happen So Fast Though We Did Have A Blast

You Constantly Making Me Laugh And That Isn't Even The
Half
No Sooner Than Later You Thought You Found Greater

Though I Know What It Really Is I Must Say That I Do Miss
The Times We Kissed
You Had Me On High My Mind Stayed In The Sky

In My Eyes You Were That Guy I Can't Deny You Did Make
Me Cry
I Didn't Have A Clue It Takes A While To Brew I Was Being
Played Like A Fool

It Didn't Happen At The Drop Of A Dime It Took Some Time
But I Got Over You My Nights Are No Longer Blue My Spirit
Feels Brand New

Had I Only Knew Prior To I Wouldn't Have Given In So Easily
but Stayed True To Me Now That it's Off My Chest I Know
How to Deal With The Rest

Won't Be A Wonder Think Or A Guess From Beginning ,
Middle And End
We'll Remain Best Of Friends

That Way We Won't Leave Each Other Blind But Our Minds
Bind To One
Now That's A True Love To Find

SO YOU SAY

Who gave you the right to tell me when I can and when I
can't
To say when I will and when I won't, how about when I come
and when I go
The last I checked and it is apparent the ones who were able
to do that were my parents
Now you can sit there, arms folded looking at me crossed
eyed, do what you want to
But I'm definitely not going to be treated as such especially
not by you

ONE DAY I PRAYED

My mind is tangled, too many decisions
The stress, I'm a mess
I shout, I know You can help me without a doubt
So I come to You for answers to straighten me out
There isn't any other way, I know Your love is here to stay
I will praise and worship You, each and everyday

MY SWEET PATRICIA

December 24, 2011, God took you Home
He needed you in Heaven

You brought the family together
every year at Christmas Eve

I Truly Believe You Held on & Fought
For This is the Day You Were Destined to Leave

I Have a Friend in You, You Have a Friend in Me
You Are the Mother I Never Had
Forever We Will Remain Family

You Treated Me just like a Daughter
I Will Miss your Beautiful Smile, Yours Hugs, Your Touch
Never will I Forget Your Last Words to Me "Annika, I Love
You So Much"

Words cannot Describe the Way I Feel
It's the wonderful memories of times we shared I'll use to Heal

You are now with your Precious Tina
No pain, No worries, Full of Strength

Calm, At Peace with serenity
Wrap your Wings around Me

Keep them there, My Guarding Angel, into Eternity you'll
always be

MENTOR

Mr. James D Evans,
My Guiding Angel sent from Heaven

My Mentor, my Motivator, my Friend
You'll hold a special place in my Heart to the end

Never steering me in the wrong direction
We will forever have this beautiful connection

To the end on earth you see
For My Love for you is Eternity

God sent you to me from Heaven
Mr. James D. Evans

TONES

No matter your Tone..we have the same color Bones..
Personalities Unique..All the Same UNDERNEATH..True
Beauty is Skin Deep..Though Our Souls are His to Keep..The
Eye of the Beholder—> Holds the KEY

THUMP

Thump, Thump, Thump, Swish, Swish, Swish was the sound of my sneakers, tapping the ground; my body moving freely, gliding round and round; my feet lightly touching on impact; thoughts in my mind remain intact; Birds guiding me, moving swiftly trying to steady my pace, Breeze slightly blowing, kissing my face; pushing it, wanting it, all 4 miles ,every inch of the way all smiles

UNDERSTAND

~HAPPY VALENTINE'S DAY~ How can one understand another who isn't willing to open up? Only the seen can be understood & the unseen perceived, therefore one can't completely be understood! Understand?? I DO!

PARADISE

MY PARADISE WITHIN ME, IS WHAT MAKES ME HAPPY, IF
YOU FEEL I'VE BEEN A NEGATIVE IN YOUR LIFE, PLEASE,
FORGIVE ME
I ASK THE LORD TO MAKE ME BETTER
LET NO MAN JUDGE ME, LEAVE THAT UP TO HE

QUEENDOM

QUEENDOM»»»A Place Where A Woman Knows She Is Beautifully Human-A Special Place She Feels Wanted-A Special Place She Knows She Is Appreciated-A Special Place She Shows Confidence-A Special Place She Wants For Nothing Yet Has Everything-A Special Place She Is Treated As She's On Top Of The World Because She Is Within Her Own Paradise-A Special Place She Feels The Love All Around Her-A Special Place She Holds Her Head Up High For She Knows She Is Beautifully Human And Fits Well In Her Special Place

SEEDS

If you CLEARLY see the visible SIGNS & RED FLAGS from
the jump, why press on like there will be CHANGE? Sure
you may keep the peace for a moment and maintain though
the seed is still planted and gets fed by the rain, the issue at
hand will grow not get rid of the pain, be wise and avoid the
misery that will drive
you insane

SNAKES

Watch out for the SNAKE that slithers behind you
He awaits to use you as a fool
The owl veering down in the tree
You are too blind to see
The shady leopard on the hilltop
He ain't never gonna change his spots
Be Aware of the Wolf in Sheep Clothing full of Hate
He wants nothing more than to keep you
From getting to the Gate

ME BECAUSE

I Am Me Because Of He
Mine, Inner Divine, Wrapped Up In
My Soul, Being, and Mind
Some Say I'm Naive, Others Say I'm Gullible
But They Haven't Walked In My Shoes Or Fought In This
Struggle
To Be Me I'm Happy Go Lucky, Peace Of Mind, Spirit Free,
I Love All That I Am, I Love ME, I'm Not Conceited By Any
Means, Down To Earth, Strong, Not Too Proud
Hold All Mine Down, Do It All With Love, Not Even a Smear
Frown
Thank The Lord For His Glory And Grace He's The One
Behind This Smile On My Face
I'm Humble That's What He Commands I Thrive To Be His
Servant Live Out His Demands, Though It Takes Patience
and Time, One Day, One Day, I Shout To The Lord
Disperse All Negativity, Help Clear My Mind, As Long As
You Know You Instilled It In My Spirit To Be Kind, They
Haven't A Clue That It Was Already Written: You Knew,
Now Unveiled My Soul, Spiritual Being, Is The Truth Of
Annika—> My Inner Divine

MISERY

~Misery LOVES company, yes indeed..If your motive is to
put anyone down or be NEGATIVE, P.L.E.A.S.E
don't come around me~

~CHOCOLATE HERSHEY SWIRL~

Down to Earth, Pretty face, Bright smile, wrapped with
Delight
I remember the first night, you extended your friendship
Your Spirit surrounded by Extreme Light

Strong, Sophisticated, Funny, Mind Free, Sweet as can be
Like Chocolate covered Strawberries, Hershey Almond
Kisses
Pleasant as nectar is to a bird, Maple is to syrup, Honey is to
a bee
Thank you for accepting me for me

True to yourself indeed,
For I know you'll be there for anyone in need

Personality Out of This World, a Gem, a Pearl
Intertwined, like a Vanilla & Chocolate Ice Cream Cone Swirl
That's Robin, My Friend, and My Girl

I WISH I MAY

I WISH I MAY I WISH I MIGHT
HAVE MY WISH COME TRUE TONIGHT
I THOUGHT OUR LOVE WAS TRUE AT FIRST SIGHT
BUT NOW I KNOW IT JUST WASN'T RIGHT
FOR THE LOVE OF ME, I CANT FIGURE OUT WHY
WE WEREN'T MEANT TO BE, THEN I REALIZED
IT WAS THE GAMES YOU PLAYED WITH ME
I WISH I MAY I WISH I MIGHT
PLEASE DON'T TAKE AWAY MY CLEAR SIGHT

STICKS & STONES

They say sticks and stones will break your bones but words
will NEVER hurt you, well THAT'S A LIE!!
Words of HATRED pierce through your heart as time flies
by,
the hole it forms underneath opens deep as you go about
your daily life,
they flow swiftly through every vein
merely making you go insane
by just the thought of what was said
can surely mess up someone's head,
think twice before you attack, spoken words are something
you can't take back

"ANNIKA" WHO SHE IS"

I really like when people tell ANNIKA what she really likes.
I really like when people tell ANNIKA what she really
wants . . . I really like when people tell ANNIKA what she's
all about...I really like when people tell ANNIKA what she
really sees...I really like when people tell ANNIKA what she
really NEEDS...I really like when people tell ANNIKA WHO
SHE REALLY LOVES!?! They don't walk the steps of ANNIKA
so how do they know...I am careful to give MY advice...
never put on a show nor an act...one thing I must say is she's
ALERT to the FACT